"With clever insight and unique perspective, Christee Goode encourages and challenges young women to explore the intimacy and depths of the Lord. Her unforgettable experiences are shared with transparent honesty and coupled with profound applications of the Word of God. Thirty Something will catapult young women into liberation as they overcome the design of the enemy and guide them as they walk into the destiny of the Lord."

Dr. Samuel R. Chand,
Chancellor, Beulah Heights Bible College and Founder of Samuel R. Chand Ministries

"Thirty Something is an amazing and enthralling testimony of Christee Goode's personal journey into the peace of God. As a woman in my thirties, I have been blessed personally by her astute insight into the Word of the Lord and what it says for us. This book is a must read for all women as we continue to seek out the plans that the Lord has for us."

Tekeita N. Lodge,
M.B.A., Human Resources Manager

30something

something

CHRISTEE T. GOODE

TATE PUBLISHING *& Enterprises*

TATE PUBLISHING
& Enterprises

Thirty Something
Copyright © 2006 by Christee Goode. All rights reserved.
Visit www.tatepublishing.com for more information.

Additional Editing by Beth Krippner
Scripture quotations marked "NLT" are taken from the Holy Bible, New Living Translation, Copyright © 1996. Used by permission of Tyndale House Publishers, Inc. All rights reserved.
Scripture quotations marked "NIV" are taken from the Holy Bible, New International Version ®, Copyright © 1973, 1978, 1984 by International Bible Society. Used by permission of Zondervan Publishing House. All rights reserved.
Scripture quotations marked "KJV" are taken from the Holy Bible, King James Version, Cambridge, 1769.
The opinions expressed by the author are not necessarily those of Tate Publishing, LLC.
This book is designed to provide accurate and authoritative information with regard to the subject matter covered. This information is given with the understanding that neither the author nor Tate Publishing, LLC is engaged in rendering legal, professional advice. Since the details of your situation are fact dependent, you should additionally seek the services of a competent professional.

Book design copyright © 2006 by Tate Publishing, LLC. All rights reserved.
Cover design by Janae Glass
Interior design by Elizabeth Mason

Published in the United States of America

ISBN: 1-5988662-0-6
06.10.13

To Mommy,
Thank you for giving me wings.

Acknowledgments

Lord I thank you so much for the guidance, wisdom, courage, and ability to write. You never cease to amaze me.

To my parents, Richard and Lois Goode, thank you for supporting me in anything and everything that I choose to do. I would not be who I am today without your constant love, guidance, wisdom, and support. I couldn't ask for better parents, so to answer your inevitable question . . . yes Dad, you are a good father!

To my big brother Troy, you have encouraged and inspired me throughout our entire lives. I love you so much. Thank you for always trying to be the best brother and the best supporter of me in all my endeavors. To my sister-in-law Theresa, you are a wonderful model as a woman of God, a mother, a wife, and a friend. I have watched you more than you think I have, and I have learned more than you know. I am eternally grateful that you joined our family and allowed me to join yours. To Troysie and Maya, Auntie Christee loves you so much! Thanks for being the sweetest and most hilarious niece and nephew team around!

To Bishop Gilbert A. Thompson and Sis. Yvonne Thompson, thank you for the covering of prayer, love, and support and for providing yet another tremendous model of holiness in my life.

To Kimberly Stotts (Kimmy Lou), thank you for the strong woman of God you are, your honesty, your openness, and your friendship.

To Maureen ("Mo") Folkes, you are such a precious friend, prayer partner, and running mate! You have been one of my biggest cheerleaders - thank you so much for always being in my corner. To Deanna Godfrey and Tekeita Lodge, thank you for the countless words of encouragement and helping me to keep this work moving! To Damon Isiah, thank you for your continuous support and encouragement.

To Tan, Andy, and Janelle, thank you for the years of friendship that I drew upon while writing. You all have been wonderful models of what God can and will do in our lives if we submit to Him. Thank you for being my sisters.

To those unmentioned, but not unnoticed, thank you for your continuous love, prayers, and support.

Table of Contents

Foreword

Brilliant, Beautiful, Focused, Multi-taskers, Ambitious and Energetic, just a few adjectives to describe those of you who hover between the ages of 25 and 40.

You are doing very well educationally, socially, relationally, economically and spiritually. However, you are still experiencing a large amount of uncertainty, questioning and even frustration as you stop and ponder who you are, where you have been, and more importantly, where you want to go.

With remarkable style, Christee Goode brilliantly describes your world in transparent fashion as she walks and lives through this same time frame (i.e., age 25–40). This exceptional book will challenge the "thirtysomethings," as well as their parents, while also showing teenagers potential potholes to avoid on their journey. Christee passes on a great advantage to the reader as she blends her spiritual Christian journey with her background in pharmacy and law by offering a prescription for healing and direction that will stand up in the court of life. Heed it, grow and be blessed.

Richard Allen Goode

The Revelation

THERE IS NOTHING WRONG WITH ME.

For years I've tried to convince myself of this, yet for years I've also struggled with feelings of jealousy and insecurity, and a lack of self-worth. Why was I inordinately envious when one of my friends accomplished something that I had not? I have celebrated with my friends through countless engagements, marriages and pregnancies, although I myself was not engaged, married or pregnant. I have mastered the language of "Oh great, I'm so happy for you." The truth is that I was not necessarily unhappy for them, but I was unhappy for me. I'm embarrassed to recount how frequently I have screamed out, "When is it my turn?"

Is this just me? I don't think so. In talking with my friends, both married and single, over the years, I have learned that many of us struggle with these feelings. This cannot be what God has planned for our lives. This cannot be what He purposed us for. I have struggled with this jealousy and insecurity tremendously for years. What I have realized is that jealousy and insecurity are simply a curse of the enemy (the devil) and nothing more. The bad news is that many of us are cursed and we don't even realize it. The good news is that curses can, and will, be broken.

The enemy's plan was to torment and destroy me with these feelings. Yet this struggle is precisely what fueled my passion for writing to you. God has given me the courage to share parts of me, including my embarrassments, mishaps and some of those pesky "skeletons" that have been hanging in my closet. My prayer is that as I share mine, you will find release from many of the same issues and struggles that the enemy has used or is using to destroy you. I pray that as you read, you will ask the Lord to open your mind and your heart to truly receive from Him. I encourage you to ask that the scales be removed from your eyes so that you may see the areas in your life in which you need release. Now, I understand that you may read parts of this book and decide that your story is not like mine, or that you would have never made some of the choices that I made. Yet, I challenge you to look past your personal judgments about me to see what God is revealing about you. There is a reason you have chosen to read this book. There are areas in your life that you have never explored, and questions that you need to ask and answer about yourself. There is so much more about you that God wants to make known to you. You are so much more than you know. There is nothing wrong with you.

I have always attracted the same type of people as close friends, and these relationships triggered my desire to write specifically to the thirtysomethings. My friends and I are rather transparent with one another. We do not compete with one another. We do not hide our embarrassments, our bad choices or our ignorance on any issue. We just love and share with one another. I have been blessed with very close friends with whom I can share some of my innermost thoughts, fears and desires. These relationships are what I draw upon as I write to you. They helped generate my courage to write this book, and I have actually found great joy in exposing myself for the world to read. The purpose of this book is to be transparent about my life in an effort and a hope that you, too, will become more transparent about yours. Granted, I am choosing to do this on a national forum, which may render me quite the laughingstock among those who know me. What you choose to do with my book is up to you. You may laugh at me, or you may find yourself in some of my writing. The one thing I know, and why God gave me the desire to write, is that we all are insecure in some form or another and part of our insecurities are fed because we are not transparent enough with one another.

In the eyes of many, the fact that I have obtained two doctorate degrees is a fantastic accomplishment. On a paper resume, or via an oral introduction, I could appear to be somewhat "together." The truth is that I am not. Now that I have exposed myself, wherever I go, there could possibly be someone there who has read my book, and because they have read it, they will know more about me than I know about them. They will know that I am not nearly as *together* as I seem on paper. If you are there, you will know my heart, my thoughts, my fears and my weaknesses. You will know me. My prayer in writing this book is simply that by knowing me with all of my craziness, flaws, imperfections and insecurities, you will learn to know yourself. When you know yourself, you will reveal yourself to others with all of *your* craziness, flaws, imperfections and insecurities. As we each begin this cycle, the curses of the enemy will be devoured. His plan to destroy so many of our spirits with feelings of jealousy, insecurity and a lack of self-worth will be conquered because we have recognized his plan and we have taken action against him. God will begin a cycle of revelation of his desires for women across the nations. We are not here to compete with one another, but to help fulfill God's plans in each other. Our transparency will help see us through. So start the cycle. You do not have to be as public as I am, but start the cycle somewhere.

Windows

While a man can make it to the gym, shower and shave, and still make it to work in just about an hour, it is never that easy for a woman. We sometimes forgo the gym simply because it does not coincide with the hairstyle that we chose for that day. Accordingly, for the sake of beauty, we tend to put excess weight on around our hips and thighs - the area that many studies show is most dangerous for our health. It is one of the more difficult equations to balance, almost as if it's a curse. Yet, despite it, there is still something fantastic about being a woman. There are still some areas that we balance extraordinarily well.

When it comes to our families, especially our men, we nurture, we support, and we will love unconditionally. We are first in line to help a man rise to his potential. Oh, that's not you? Well it certainly has been me. I have "worked with a brotha" in many ways. I have dated them with no job, a sorry job, just lost a job, can't find a job, and can't keep a job. No kids, one kid and maybe two kids. No drama, minor drama, and sometimes major drama. You get my point. I have had my share.

I have been loving and supportive, but over the years I have learned something about myself. Yes, I will love hard, and I will try to "work with a man." Yet once the relationship is over, it's done and that's the end of it. I will cry until my eyelids have swollen to twice their size, but I will not go back. It's what I call the cut-off point. Many of us have one. While it may seem harsh to just cut someone out of my life, trust me - those relationships needed to be cut off. Now I certainly can forgive, but *forgive* is not synonymous with *return*, so I do not go back. I see it as though God opened a window for me, and I jumped out. That is one of my strengths; I know when to jump.

Jumping isn't an easy thing to do, especially when you're older and time doesn't appear to be in your favor. I've even heard a well-known minister preach that if you have a good man, you'd better work to keep him because there aren't that many out there. Well, thank you very much, but I am not going to stay with a man that I'm not married to just because he is a man. He may even be a semi-decent man, but if he's not the man that God has for me, I cannot stay. If God opens a window for me, I have to jump.

I have dated men who have been *kind enough* to remind me of my age as if to tell me that my chances of marriage and children are getting slim. I even dated a man who declared that I wasn't likely going to do better than he. He politely informed me that *all* men are conniving and dishonest. Now, I will admit that hearing these things can certainly cause fear to start creeping into your heart as it did mine. You may not realize it, but those words and ideas can also begin to diminish your confidence. It sounds silly, but if you hear those words often enough, you may actually start to believe that perhaps you *cannot* do better, so perhaps you should stay. This happens to the best of us. You may be the most educated woman on the block, but if you look at the empirical data available, it points to your slim chances at finding love as well.

The Statistics Show . . .

Ah yes, the statistics. We have to stop being afraid of that data. Those statistics are the result of someone's job. There's a statistician out there somewhere calculating these figures for us. We don't know this person, but we rely on him (or her!) to tell us what our chances are for marriage and childbirth. We rely on this person to relay to us what our chances are for happiness. Well, I have decided that I am no longer relying on that person. I am no longer afraid of that data, nor am I afraid to jump out of an open window.

I have lived in three major cities: Miami, Atlanta, and Boston. Despite what you may have heard about where the men are, I did not get closest to marriage until I got to Boston. In fact, I was three months away from the altar when the Lord opened a window for me. I had become consumed with turning thirty and I was determined to get married. I had met a seemingly nice Christian gentleman who was just a few years older than I. Now, I am definitely guilty of the typical marriage planning after the first date. (Don't laugh. You probably are, too.) That is exactly what I did in this case. I had an idea of a fairy-tale romance. We would date for a very brief period, become engaged, and get married. We had almost succeeded with my plan when God interrupted with His. Not only had I become afraid that this was my only chance for marriage, but I had stopped listening to the Lord and started listening to everyone else around me, including that statistician (the one I had never met). I will admit that the major problem in that relationship was me. I had gotten to a place in my singleness where I was practically begging the Lord to bring someone into my life. I cried quite frequently at night, and I dreaded returning to my empty home alone. My personal desire for marriage had become an unknowing obsession. Well, that wasn't my first time, but it certainly was my last time to beg God for anyone or anything!

What about you? Are you obsessing or desiring something so badly that you are willing to take anything? You have to date in order to get married, so I don't think I was in error for dating this man. The problem was that I did not allow the Lord to work according to *His* time. I laced up my running shoes, I set my mark, the gun fired, and this runner was off! Fortunately for me (and all of us), God is a faithful protector. Just hours before I signed a contract for my wedding, the Lord revealed what was, in my opinion, a major character flaw in this man. One which I could not accept.

That night I was given a choice to either continue to pursue my desires, or to jump out the window. I jumped. Sometimes God opens a door wide and sometimes it's just a window. Whichever way, the Lord *always* gives us the choice. Evaluate your current relationships. You may need to open your eyes to see if the Lord has opened a window for you. God is faithful and he will make a way of escape for you. See *1 Corinthians 10:13*. Don't be afraid to jump.

Intimacy with God

We often stay in relationships that clearly require an exit strategy. Why do we continue to date a man when we know there's no future or hope with him? I have stayed several times, trying to create something out of nothing. I knew in my heart that he was not the one, so why did I stay? Usually out of fear. But why are we afraid to walk away? We're so afraid of what is "out there" or even that there may be nothing out there for us. We think, "I don't want to be single again; I don't want to be back in that boat. I want to get married because I'm getting too old. What will everyone say or think?" One of my biggest fears was that I would have to watch all of my friends, sorority sisters and relatives get married before I did. Well, guess what? I have basically watched it all happen. This means that I am currently living out my biggest fear. What I have realized is that, actually, the reality isn't that bad after all! I think that old cliché is actually correct: *That which does not kill us only makes us stronger.* Seeing as though I am definitely not dead, I suppose that means I'm one strong woman! I like to think so.

There is another fear that some of us still face and must be exposed. It is the fear of what we may be giving up in order to find an intimate relationship with the Lord. A major problem for women, especially Christian women, is the struggle with *giving up sex.* We either ignore what we're doing by having sex or we ignore what it is doing to us. Surprisingly, I still hear the same arguments today to justify a "sexual" Christian lifestyle that many of us made years ago. People still assume they are giving up something by truly denying themselves in order to follow Christ. I've heard it all before: "I have needs and my man has needs, and I am not going to let any other women come in and fulfill his needs in my place. If I don't give it to him, someone else will." Oh, I know that argument, because I have relied upon it myself. It's time to let it go. Have you ever thought about why we have those needs? The only reason we *think* we need sex is because we have had it before. Think about it: If you were a virgin, you would not know what being with a man was like. You would not know what it is like to wake up next to a man that you think you are in love with. How can you miss something that you have never had? You could only wish for something that you have heard about, but you could never miss it or feel as though you were giving it up.

For those of us who are not virgins, we have already tested the waters of marriage, without the commitment, of course, so we know how beautiful it is supposed to be. Yet there is one thing we did not count on. We did not count on the guilt and the shame that come along with the territory. We did not count on the jealousy and the insecurities that would follow. This is a tough pill to swallow and one we often choose to ignore, but the truth is that being in a sexual relationship with a man that you are not married to opens up voids in our lives that can *never* be filled by him. They were only meant for your husband. Now that those areas are open, they have to be filled somehow, so what happens? Guilt, insecurities, jealousies, loneliness, diseases, pregnancies and miscarriages - these all fill the voids. So remind me . . . what were we giving up again?

Do not be afraid to live out your greatest fear. It may spark the greatest relationship that you've ever known - a relationship with the Lord. Let the Lord into your life when you are single, afraid and free. Let Him in while there is no one else there occupying your heart, your mind or your time. Get to know the

Lord and the power of His resurrection and the fellowship of His suffering. See *Philippians 3:10.* Get to that place in your heart in which you crave Him and you want nothing more than His presence in your life. You can feel His presence even in a crowded room; you can hear His voice gently reassuring you of his love for you. You feel the tears starting to well up in your eyes because His presence is so overwhelming in your heart. He is so real that you can almost touch Him. His voice is so audible that you can hear every word as if he is physically standing right next to you. He is so powerful that you do not want to ever lose this feeling. You are in love, and that is intimacy. It is the purest form of love. There is no guilt or shame in this love. There is no bitterness, no jealousy and no envy in this love. This is God's love. This is intimacy with God. It took me so long to get to this place with the Lord because I was afraid. If you are twenty-, thirty- or sixty-something, do not be afraid of finding this intimacy with the Lord. Give your hearts to the Lord and receive His love.

Once you receive this love, show your love for Him in the same way you show others. When you're dating, how do you express your affection? When you're really in love with someone, what do you do? When I am in love, I tend to make myself available to that person. I will rearrange my entire schedule, just to make time for him. Well, that is now my promise to the Lord. Because I am in love with Him, I will rearrange my schedule for Him. I will make time for Him every day. God doesn't want some bogus sacrifice; do not come to Him at the end of the day with your leftovers after you have given your best to everyone and everything else all day. He wants your first fruits. He wants your Abel sacrifice, not your Cain sacrifice. God plays "seconds" to no one and nothing. *"You will seek me and find me when you seek me with all of your heart. I will be found by you, declares the Lord . . ." Jeremiah 29:13–14, NIV.* He wants to be found by you. Start seeking Him. *"Seek the Lord while he may be found, call on him while he is near." Isaiah 55:6, NIV.* As you seek Him, He will reveal so much about Himself to you. It is too hard to stay depressed when you are reading His Word over and over. It is too hard to be lazy when you read what is available to you. It is too hard to stay angry when you read how loving God is. It is too hard to hold grudges when you read how forgiving he is.

A relationship with God is just like a relationship with anyone else you love. Some days you love that person so much that you just cannot get enough of them and you want to be with them all day. Then there are days when you still love that person, but it is not as emotional and you are not as expressive. That is how I am with God. Some days, I am on fire and I can feel his presence so much stronger than on other days. Then on some days I love Him, but because I get so caught up in the intricacies of life, I do not stop to love Him like I should. Now, I strive not to only *feel* good when God is giving me "stuff," or things are falling into place (although those are good days, too). I strive to love him the same way he loves me, unconditionally.

Learn how to worship the Lord, like He is your husband and your best friend. Learn how to love Him the way He wants to be loved. Learn how to be intimate with God. Love him. Once you love Him, you will trust Him. Once you trust Him, you will learn to live without fear, and you will grow and evolve into the completeness that God has designed for you. Invest in this transformation so you can become complete in God.

Pray with me: *God, I am so in love with you. You are everything to me. Apart from you, Lord, I can do nothing and I am nothing. Oh, how I praise your majestic name! You are so holy, Lord; you are so worthy, Lord; you are so faithful, Lord; and you are so loving, Lord. I love you with all of my heart, all of my mind, and all of my soul. I will serve you, Lord, and you alone. I will put nothing else before you. I will live my life in total devotion to you.*

Man's Rejection Is God's Protection

I have been rejected by my fair share of men. By rejection I mean that they broke off a relationship with me, they weren't interested to start, or they included others in our relationship without my knowledge. Oftentimes, when a man gives priority to someone or something else, for me, it is a form of rejection. I dated a man once who was dating me, along with another young woman. I gave him an ultimatum, and a few years later, I saw him *and* his wife at a mutual friend's wedding. I dated another man I thought I surely would marry, but two years into the relationship, he still had not found me to be a suitable wife. Another boyfriend of mine made some terrible choices in his behavior with other women while dating me. Hey, don't laugh! Your dating record probably isn't that great, either! While I'm getting pretty good at recognizing when to jump out of the windows God has opened for me, the area that I still struggle with is dealing with what happens next. Something goes wrong in the relationship, and I tend to internalize the problem, assuming it was something to do with me. Shortly after my exodus from a relationship, the feelings of rejection begin to settle in. Typically a pattern of self-doubt and questioning - "What's wrong with me?" tends to coincide with that rejection.

My Bishop often repeats to women who have gotten out of relationships, or who have not been pursued by some man, that "man's rejection is God's protection." While that has a nice ring to it, it's not so easy to grab onto that belief when you are smack-dab in the middle of your rejection period. So what do you do? You say it anyway. Say it in your head and aloud, over and over: *Man's rejection is God's protection.* Repeat it daily, even hourly if you need to, until it resonates in your ears. You say it as tears are rolling down your face, you write it down, you leave it by your bed, and you stick it in your desk at work. You repeat it as much as you need to until it slowly starts to make sense to you and gradually you begin to believe that it really is true. It is painful to feel rejected, but you have to believe that God is always protecting you *from* something or protecting you *for* something that you just cannot see.

You may feel rejected by a former love or even a parent. If your earthly father has never truly been a part of your life, you may feel as though he has rejected you. Yet, his rejection may actually have served you better in becoming who you are today. I say this because we are all very much a product of the environment that we were raised in. Perhaps your father would not have been able to raise you to become what God wants you to become. I believe that God takes the best qualities from our parents and gives them to the offspring. Sometimes, by being in the presence of your parents, you learn some of the negative traits and qualities that God never meant for you to have. Perhaps your absent father would have taught you how to be selfish, or to think negatively. Perhaps he would have demonstrated how to cheat, steal or lie your way through life. His rejection of you is not based on anything wrong that you did or said. God used his rejection of you for your own protection.

You have to believe in God's love and mercy in order to understand this protection. You have to believe that you are God's precious child in order to understand why you have to hurt right now. The pain you have felt or are feeling now is only temporary, but God has so much more in store for you. It hurts, but believe it. *"'Because he loves me', says the Lord, 'I will rescue him; I will protect him, for he acknowledges my name. He will call upon me, and I will answer him; I will be with him in trouble, I will deliver him and honor him. With long life will I satisfy him and show him my salvation'" Psalm 91:14–15, NIV.*

Reflect over a previous period of your life when God protected you. Remind yourself of the pain and how the Lord healed you in the past. Trust Him that He will do it again for you. This present-day situation is no more difficult for God. Nothing is too hard for God. When God protects you from something or someone, it may be painful for a moment. This is part of the fire in which we all must be tried, but when we come out, we are certainly as pure as gold. God has a purpose for your life, and in all likelihood, that man would have been a hindrance for you in fulfilling this purpose. Nothing will stop God's plan for your life, unless *you* allow it.

Moving Forward

There is always going to be someone who is prettier than you, who is smarter than you, who has more money than you, who dresses better than you, who is funnier than you, or who has more talent than you. *Always.* You have to learn to find peace with what God created in you. Honestly, with whom would you want to trade places? My answer to that question that I have often asked myself is always emphatically *no one.* That must count for something. That has to mean that I like, maybe even love, myself, right? If this is true for you also, we have to stop this continuous struggle with rejection, emptiness and insecurity. I am tired of not truly celebrating with others in their time of joy. I am exhausted with this constant comparison of my life with theirs. I am tired of leaving a fellowship with others, only to go silently into my own space to sit in misery and pity. Aren't you? It stops now.

The funny thing about the devil is that even as I typed those words, he tried to discourage me. I heard him saying, "No one is going to read this, publish this or care about what you have to say." For one moment, I felt rather silly for writing these thoughts down. Then I remembered the purpose of the book. We all share so many of these same feelings and the enemy wants us to believe that we are ridiculous and alone in this struggle. If we believe the thoughts the enemy places in our heads more than we believe what the Word of the Lord says, we will never be delivered. We will live our lives in a constant competition, never finding true peace with God or ourselves. Well, I am stepping up to the plate to embarrass myself, my friends and my family (sorry, guys!). Yes, it is embarrassing to admit that you have felt rejected and you have been jealous of someone you love, care about or do not even know. It is embarrassing to reveal that you may smile a lot or make people laugh, but you secretly struggle and are often tormented by your own thoughts and insecurities. We have to admit these types of feelings to discover their origin, deal with them and ultimately conquer them. We have to admit them to God, to one another and to ourselves in order to find our deliverance. We have to learn that man's rejection is truly for our protection and stop analyzing the rejection as though something is wrong with us. If you think something is wrong with you, you cannot find peace with yourself, and you certainly cannot pray for others or be happy for them.

We have to learn to truly celebrate with others in their victories and genuinely pray with them through their trials. Read the story of Job. The Word says that Job prayed for his friends and he was blessed. See *Job 42:10*. Of all people, Job needed prayers the most, but he truly prayed for the blessings of his friends, and ultimately he was blessed. We have to learn to have the heart of Job. This doesn't mean to just start rambling off ineffective and miscellaneous prayers for people. Empty and meaningless words are just that - they mean nothing. This means honest, sincere and fervent prayers. Just try it by starting with something small. If your friend really needs a new car, pray for her to get a new car, even though you may not be happy with the car you drive or the bus you ride. Start with the small prayers. During your time of rejection, hurt and pain, it may be hard to see others being blessed in front of you, but the truth is, it is harder to see them suffer. Recognize that you feel rejected, then recognize the source of the feeling. Examine how that feeling is affecting your attitudes toward others. As you learn to sincerely pray for others and celebrate with them, even during your time of need, the Lord will give you peace and deliverance. The Lord has protected you more times than you realize, and this temporary period is just that - temporary. Man's rejection is God's protection. Whatever you feel right now, ask the Lord to give you the heart of Job. *"Create in me a clean heart, O God. Renew a right spirit within me" Psalm 51:10, KJV.*

Pray with me: *I love you, Lord, and you are the Lord of my life. I know that any man's rejection of me is without a doubt your mercy and protection from something that I can't quite see. Lord, you have protected me for a purpose and I am going to trust you to fulfill that purpose in my life. I recommit my life to you. I will not be impatient, I will not be discouraged, and I will no longer feel rejected. I trust you and I know that you have my best interests in mind, so I will continue to believe that you are working everything out for my good. Man's rejection is God's protection. Amen.*

Alone is not Alone

Sometimes at night I make a cup of my favorite chamomile tea or hot chocolate and prepare to settle in for the evening. I sit quietly in my home and laugh at how much my life will soon change. As of now, the only noise I hear at night is the occasional neighbor, my teapot whistling, or the noise from the train that runs alongside my street. Other than that, if my television is off and I am not on the phone, there is silence. In my experience, silence can invoke either loneliness or peace. I choose peace. Which do you choose? Are you the type of woman who keeps her television set turned on at all times, or has to have friends over, or someone to talk to on the phone? Are you the type to do whatever you have to, just to avoid the silence? That was often the case for me in the past. I learned to entertain myself somehow, just to keep from being reminded that I was alone. Now I choose peace. I have to wonder, during evenings like these, if these are the times that married women are referring to when they say, "Enjoy your singleness." Yes, it can be lonely at times, but this is only temporary. Stop fighting your few moments of alone time. While it may seem like a lifetime, under God's time, it is only a few moments. Your life is going to change, but do not fixate on that. Just be still and enjoy those moments of peace. Do not be afraid to be alone, even if it is only for a few moments. Do not be afraid of what you may realize about yourself if you are alone. Sometimes we cloud and crowd ourselves with the lives of others, but Paul said, *"I have learned to be content whatever the circumstances" Philippians 4:11, NIV.* Learn to be content with yourself and by yourself.

You may be afraid to spend time alone, but I challenge you not to fear what you have not embraced. I have a rather strange analogy, but I think it works: I can compare this with foods that I have never tried. I grew up in Indiana, what I affectionately deem the land of "no culture." Moving to Miami and then Boston (with Atlanta and Tallahassee in between) exposed me to so much diversity, and with a diverse people come diverse foods. I have to tell you that I was not a fan of anything curried, just because of how it looked. I have never been one to eat things that I could not clearly see and with curry, I just was not sure what I was getting. Even writing this I realize how ungrounded my fear was. I have to admit that the first few times I tried curry, I still was not a big fan of it, but that was partly because I was still hung up on my fears and concerns. The more I tasted it, however, the more I began to love it. Now it is one of my preferred meals. Isn't that funny? Something that I was determined not to eat became something I crave. (I told you it was a strange analogy, but you get my point).

That is how we travel through life; we are afraid of what we have not tried. We are so afraid to be alone that we constantly surround ourselves with someone or something. We are constant "busy-bodies." Yet we wonder why we cannot hear from the Lord. We are too busy hearing from other people. *"Be still and know that I am God" Psalm 46:10, NIV.* That means sit still and be quiet until you hear from the Lord. He is not going to shout over your numerous phone calls, or push through the line of friends that you keep around you at all times. He is not going to wait until your favorite television program has gone off the air. He is going to wait until you are still and until you seek him. *"Search for the Lord and his strength, and keep on searching" Psalm 105:4, NLT. "He rewards those who diligently seek him" Heb 11:6, KJV. "Everyone who seeks, finds" Matthew 7:8, NLT.* Search the pages of the Word to find Him and His love. Keep seeking, asking and knocking and the door will be opened to you. You have to have quiet time with the Lord. Quiet your spirit and do not think about the previous day or the days to come. Clear your mind so the Lord can renew your mind. Do not waste your life away running from this position to that position and from this meeting to that meeting. "I'm on this committee and that committee, and I do this, and this, and that." Don't make your primary goal your resume, or even worse - your obituary. Be still! Now, more than ever, is the time to focus on the Lord and His plans for your life. I know it is hard, especially when so many others seem to have all their ducks lined up in a row, but you have to run the race that has been set before you. Be quiet and be still.

Insecurity Exposed

I write for both you and me, because I have struggled, I have feared, and I often have been insecure. I have found myself fearing what people think of me, and often been afraid that someone will stumble across the realization that my life is not as "put together" as I would like them to believe. This is especially true when I catch someone glancing at my unoccupied ring finger; I immediately assume that they are making assumptions about me. I detest the thought of being labeled as just another single sister who probably cannot keep a man or is just too picky. I hate the fact that being single is often viewed as some disease, which all married women must immediately pity. There are many of us who feel this way. We are either consumed by an image we feel we need to portray, or we are determined to convince the people around us that everything is okay. I have learned that I was often falsely assuming that someone was "thinking" about me. The truth is that no one is trying to figure me or my life out. No one really cares. As for the few who do, they care only for the purpose of indulging in a few moments of gossip. In all likelihood, their own lives are probably so miserable that they feel the need to find fault with someone else. Unfortunately I know this scenario all too well because I have also been that person. Embarrassingly, I must admit that I have often hoped that others are not as happy as they seem because that would make my life seem a bit more in order.

This fear about what others think is one consequence of pride - our sense of value, achievement or self-worth. The answers we scramble to respond with when asked to describe who we are or where we are going. We live our lives in search of something to be proud of or for someone to be proud of us. For awhile, I tried to keep to myself and stay out of the limelight. I wouldn't go to certain events or places because I didn't want to have to reveal that yes, I am still single; yes, I am back in school; yes, I have an insurmountable amount of student loan debt, or anything else that was or was not going on with me. I was avoiding facing that mental checklist that you note in your head when meeting someone new, talking to family, or catching up with someone from the past. The repertoire goes something like this:

"How have you been?" *Check.*
"What are you up to?" *Check.*
"Where are you working?" *Check.*
"Are you married yet?" *Red light! Red light! Abandon ship!*

I felt I had nothing to be proud of. Looking back, I realize how ridiculous I was. I was a pharmacist, soon to be attorney, and I was still searching for something to be proud of. That is proof that material desires and accomplishments can never satisfy us in the same way that a true relationship with the Lord will. I was searching for pride, my own worth and value based on what the world tells me is valuable and worthwhile. However, it is often that same world that will declare that I have yet to achieve my true purpose if I am not married or have not yet given birth - regardless of how many degrees I have obtained. So why do we continue our fruitless efforts to please this world?

What I was searching for was actually my fundamental problem - myself. If I were not so caught up in pride, then I would never worry about what others think of me or whether others are thinking about me at all. I wanted the stamp of approval from my family, my friends, and the world. Receiving their nod of approval would in turn provide me with the self-satisfaction I was so desperately seeking. That is pride in its rawest form.

Insecurity is deeply rooted in pride. The less I felt self-accomplished, the more I felt insecure. They walk hand-in-hand, pride and insecurity, and they are both sinful and destructive to our lives. Pride is destructive because it prevents us from pleasing God. Pride interferes with our relationship with God and it blocks our intimacy with Him. We cannot be intimate with God if we are in competition with Him and we are competing by trying to be what we want to be instead of what *He* wants us to be. We cannot truly seek the Lord and His will for our lives if we are also trying to seek our own will. That is serving two masters, both man and God, which is strictly forbidden by the Word of God. *See Matthew 6:24.*

So what does this mean for us? For me, this did not mean that I needed to drop out of law school and go become a mission worker in the fields somewhere. You may be on a similar course with a successful career or some other "grand" accomplishment. This does not necessarily mean to drop out of that race. This just means to face your fears. For me, I had to determine what those fears were. One of mine was that everyone would know that I am not *put together.* Although my resume spoke volumes of experience and achievements, my intangible resume was a mess. I did not want everyone to know that although I have two graduate degrees, I "carry myself" well, and I come from a "good" home - I was an insecure mess. That was my fear and I am facing it by pouring out my heart to you.

Pride and insecurity creep into our lives in many other not-so-obvious ways. For example, many of us suffer from tremendous credit card debt, mainly because we have no discipline. We shop every week for new outfits instead of saving, investing or paying off our other bills. I have started observing the behaviors of those who are truly wealthy (not superficially wealthy), and they tend to wear the same outfit over and over. They never seem to get caught up in the latest trends of fashion. They never wear their wealth. Guess what? It's really okay to wear the same outfit to work more than once. It's really okay if every single bag or belt does not match with just the right shoe. We are obsessed with making ourselves proud by the way we look, dress and speak that we forget to please God. We are so busy seeking the approval of others by what we do and who we have become that we forget to acknowledge that the Lord is God, He made us, and we are His. *See Psalm 100:3.* I realize that many of us, especially African-Americans, will make more money than our parents ever could have dreamed of making at our ages, but that factor is not the green light for purchasing more than our parents could have dreamed, either. We have not yet entered the Promised Land just because we can charge a new outfit, or lease a brand-new car.

Make this your year to become debt-free, or at least to get started with a plan. One method is to organize your debts from the largest to the smallest, and start paying them off one by one. It's really okay to go this season without the newest winter boots, if the boots from last year are still in good shape. If not, invest in a can of $2.99 shoe polish and whip them into shape yourself! Stop fearing what others think and break free from that mold of pride. Your pride and insecurities are likely keeping you in debt, and that is certainly not God's plan for your life. Please God this year in your finances and stop pleasing yourself by giving into those desires to spend and spend some more. It's okay if you tell your friends and family that this year you will not be buying lavish Christmas or birthday gifts because you will have to place them on your credit card. Yes, this means that they may realize that you have credit card debt, but this begins the cycle of release. By telling them, you are releasing yourself from that secret bondage. The enemy loves to destroy you and keep you bound by your own secrets. Break the secret and you will break the bondage.

We are prideful because we fear what others will think of us, so we strive for what everyone deems as success. We try to find it in the degrees we obtain, the jobs we seek, the clothes we wear, the cars we drive, and the homes we build. We seek to please ourselves and others because we are afraid of what happens if we do not. We worry about what we will eat, drink and wear. The Word of the Lord says to *"seek first his kingdom and his righteousness, and all these things will be given to you as well"* Matthew 6:33, NIV. Yet we refuse to seek God first, instead opting to create our own kingdom. Our kingdom has become our pride, as evidenced by everything that is tangible. Thus we are slowly becoming an abomination to the Lord. Take inventory of your life, your debt, your finances, your closets and your habits. Have your desires become your needs? Have you created your own kingdom, or are you truly seeking God's kingdom for your life? Release yourself from the bondage of pride and insecurity this year.

Pray with me: *Lord, I surrender my life, my fears, my finances, my habits, my desires, my needs, my wants, and my pride over to you. I commit my life to seeking your Kingdom and not my own. Lord, I seek after your will for my life. I seek after your approval, and not the approval of man. I commit my life to you again. Amen.*

Killing You Softly

It's funny how you can receive an amazing word on a Sunday morning, and while your emotions are high, you think that you will never lose that feeling. Yet you do lose it. The enemy begins to attack you the moment you have a revelation. He does not want you to hear it in the first place and he certainly does not want you to cultivate the word. Jesus warned us that the enemy comes only to steal, kill and destroy us. *See John 10:10.* Now he may try to literally kill you by connecting you with the wrong people, so that you are in the wrong place, but at his right time. However, because of God's great mercy, the devil is normally unsuccessful in this attempt, thus he resorts to trying to kill you slowly. His plan is to kill you little by little, day by day. He is subtle, he is extremely clever, and he knows our weaknesses.

He may try to kill you by using your own family. For example, if you do not get along and you do not work together as a family, he will tear you further and further apart. He may introduce you to the wrong person who will then pull you away from your family in order to isolate you from your familial support and those who may truly love and accept you as you are. He injects jealousy into the relationships between siblings, between spouses, and even between a parent and a child. How often is a wife elevated to higher positions than her husband, or a sister over a brother or vice versa? The devil tends to wave the other person's successes and accomplishments around like a banner, strategically planting seeds of jealousy and envy. If that doesn't work, he will destroy families over money issues. How many times have you heard of a family arguing over the estate of their parents or grandparents? It is often worth only a few thousand dollars, but we destroy years of building family relationships for this small amount.

If the enemy is unsuccessful with his familial attempts to kill you, he attempts to kill you through yourself. You are his greatest weapon and sometimes your own worst enemy when you allow the enemy to use you against yourself. How does he do this? Here come those pesky insecurities again. He stops at nothing. He will try to kill you with the physical insecurities that you harp on: your weight, height, scars, moles, hips, thighs, breasts, hair, teeth and face! If you love the way you look (although I haven't met many women who do), he moves on to another area in which he knows you struggle. He will surround you with people who seem to know more than you, think differently than you, or who you wish you were more like. If that doesn't work, he will constantly remind you of your failures and bad choices. He may remind you again and again of your sexual escapades that you desperately want to forget. He will blame you for the father, uncle, or family friend who *touched* you when you were simply living the life of a child. He will hold that previous abortion (or abortions) over your head until it becomes an unbearably heavy weight that you eventually decide to accept and adjust to carrying.

He never forgives your past. His plan is to serve as a constant reminder of your past, in any way that he can. He stops at nothing to kill you, to kill your spirit, to kill your drive, to kill your will to live and do something, anything for God. The enemy wants you to believe that you are not worthy to do anything for the Lord because of your past. He wants you to sit quietly on your gifts and talents rather than use them in the Kingdom. He keeps you quiet by making you feel unworthy. He will kill you and while it seems as though he is killing you softly, in truth his methods speak volumes. He is no longer subtle with his plans, in fact, he is quite blatant.

So how do you stop dying and start living again? The Word says to *"be self-controlled and alert. Your enemy the devil prowls around like a roaring lion looking for someone to devour. Resist him, standing firm in the faith, because you know that your brothers throughout the world are undergoing the same kind of sufferings"* 1 Peter 5: 8–9, NIV.

First alert yourself to the schemes and methods of the enemy. Determine where he attacks you, recognizing that he will often change his game plan. Whenever I am not worried about getting married and I am in a state of contentment in my singleness, that is when the devil starts to attack my purpose for God. He tries to show me where I am out of line with God and how it is impossible that what I am doing now is going to benefit the Kingdom. He tells me I have wasted too much time on useless things, educational pursuits and past relationships to now be used in the Kingdom. He tells me I am really not needed in the Kingdom because I have no true gifts to share and that I cannot really make a difference. I hear him, not softly, but quite loudly in my ear, and quite frequently. He is so predictable because the moment that I have recognized what he is doing and I trample over those seeds of doubt that he attempted to plant, he switches his game plan and starts reminding me of how most of my friends are married with children and that I'm not even close! That's how his relentless cycle starts all over again. The point of this illustration is so you realize it's not just you he attacks this way. He does it to me and millions more.

We have to realize that he is relentless in his efforts to kill us. How many women have turned to abusing alcohol, cigarettes or drugs because of his constant tormenting? How many have committed suicide at his command, or slept with a man because he convinced them that no one else would ever want them? He has killed so many of us and is still after you and me. We have to recognize how he kills us daily. He doesn't work once or twice a year; he works every single second of every day, tirelessly, relentlessly and ruthlessly. He is your worst enemy and you must recognize that he is your only enemy. *"For our struggle is not against flesh and blood, but against the rulers, against the authorities, against the powers of this dark world and against the spiritual forces of evil in the heavenly realms" Ephesians 6:12, NIV.*

The people you think are your enemies are not. Your boss, your associates, your old friends, your new friends, your coworkers, your siblings - they are not your enemy. The devil is the only enemy that you have. Once you think you have cleared him out of your life in one area, the Word says that he comes back seven times stronger! *See Matthew 12: 43–45.* We cannot afford to deal with him lightly and roll over and play dead every time he attacks us in our lives. Grab your weapon so that he can no longer surprise you. Your weapon is God's Word, the knowledge of that Word, and the realization of who you are through his Word. You have to know that you are more than a conqueror through Jesus Christ who loves you. *See Romans 8:37.* You have to know that the Word of God is a shield and a sword in the time of trouble. You have to know that the Word is with God, and the Word is God. *See John 1:1.* You have to know Him. You have to know God's Word or the enemy will succeed in killing you. There will not always be a minister nearby to pray for you, lay hands on you, or provide the appropriate scripture in every situation. You have to learn the Word of God for yourself. *"In fact, though by this time you ought to be teachers, you need someone to teach you the elementary truths of God's word all over again. You need milk, not solid food! Anyone who lives on milk, being still an infant, is not acquainted with the teaching about righteousness. But solid food is for the mature, who by constant use have trained themselves to distinguish good from evil" Hebrews 5: 12–14, NIV.*

It is time for us to move from milk to meat! That's why the enemy is killing us; he is no babe when it comes to his plans, yet we are like babes when it comes to God's plan for our lives. You cannot walk into your destiny if you do not take the time to learn what that destiny is. You can only learn it by spending time with the Lord. You can only learn Him by seeking His face daily.

Playtime with God and the devil is over, especially in the church. The enemy is killing us because we treat church as if it is the club. We pick out our outfits, we come to show it off, and we dance around shouting all Sunday morning long. Yet we don't really think much about God or spend any quality time with Him for the rest of the week until Bible study or the following Sunday. We are drinking milk, and that is a ritual, a habit and a tradition which the devil is using to kill us. Do not miss the intimacy or the passion of God. It is often found in your quiet time spent alone with the Lord. Break into the Word of God as you never have before, and break into your destiny.

Greener Grass

For my thirtieth birthday, I went with a group of friends on a spa retreat weekend. We really didn't want to spend the amount of money required, so our "spas" consisted of taking an extra-long, hot shower. Nevertheless, it was our girls' weekend and we just wanted to spend time together. It was a great weekend for all of us, but there was one moment in the room when I felt as though I had nothing. I was the only person in the group who wasn't married, and when the discussion turned to their husbands and marriage, I couldn't relate at all and for a moment, I was lost in resentment. I'm still not sure if I was angry that they had what I thought I wanted or if I was just angry that they shared a bond that, for the first time in our lives, I was not a part of.

I have been in that type of situation before, as I'm sure many of you have. It has happened among my friends but also around my own family. While I love spending time with my family, at the same time there are some aspects of it that I hate. While I'm an adult, I often still feel like a child or like I don't "fit in" when I am with them. I'm sure many of you have also felt this way at family gatherings and holidays. Most of the conversations are centered on their marriage and children or someone else's marriage and children. I usually can't relate to this chitchat or the experiences they have simply because I'm not in the same place in my life. I don't have to struggle to balance work and my children. I don't have to deal with who is going to pick up the kids from school, or whether I'm making the right choices for my family. I do have my own struggles and balances that I am dealing with, but I'm often left feeling as though mine just can't possibly be as crucial because I'm still single. Interestingly, these experiences have shown me that oftentimes the people you should be closest to can become foreigners to you, and you to them. I have often left a wedding or holiday gathering feeling as though my friends or family can't possibly know or understand me when they've never had to live as a single, thirtysomething-year-old, Christian woman. Yet at the same time, I cannot find fault with them for not understanding. Our lives are different, and believe it or not, differences are usually good.

It's not about trying to "fit in" or trying to make someone else understand you or stop pitying you. It's just about understanding and accepting that your lives are different, but that one is *certainly* not better than the other. There are equally good days and bad days to go around. To the extent that I am single and thirtysomething, my friends and family will never be in my shoes, and wherever they are in their lives right now, I will never be in theirs. We're just different.

Pull yourself out of that slump and start embracing the good and the bad that comes along with your singleness. It will likely follow you into a marriage just the same. Believe that one day your home will also be filled with children, family and laughter, but only in God's time. Instead of fighting to convince everyone around you that you are happy and single, begin to listen, observe and learn. This obsession with marriage and children that we often carry can creep into the relationships with our families and friends. But once we acknowledge it, we can be freed from the bitterness and envy that are desperately trying to destroy those relationships. That obsession is likely magnifying the differences between your life and theirs, leading you to believe that your life is not as good as it could be, if only you were married. I have since realized that even when I am surrounded by *my* husband and *my* children, there will undoubtedly be times of sadness and loneliness. Why should it be any different while I'm still single? The grass is never actually greener on the other side.

One of my married girlfriends unknowingly reminded me of this principle once. She is in her late twenties and she called me while she was going through what I call the "quarter-life crisis." You know, that phase where you first start questioning the Lord and your life, saying, "What am I doing? What is your plan for my life, God?" However, she was also questioning whether she married the right man, or should have married at all - thus confirming once again for me that the grass is definitely not always greener. Whether you are married or single, the challenges of life do not discriminate. They do not magically disappear once you switch the Miss to a Mrs. Sometimes they dramatically increase. That's why it's essential that you do not give up on God, and do not take issues into your own hands and step outside of the will of God in finding a mate. My girlfriend talked so candidly with me about her marriage and its difficulties, as well as the beauty of it. Whether you're single or married, you need couples like that in your life who are willing to be transparent about their homes. I love that she calls me and continues to share with me from her marriage experiences. Sometimes she seeks out my opinion or advice. She could easily dismiss my thoughts because I'm unmarried, yet she has never made any reference to my singleness. You know, those comments such as, "You'll see what I mean once you get married," or the ever-dreadful, "You're not married, so you don't understand." While I'm never happy when my friends are struggling with something, I thank God for the openness of my relationships. See, there's that cycle of transparency again. My friend had no idea that in the midst of her issues she actually ministered to me. I have learned how not to envy them or their lives and truly appreciate where I am in mine. Hopefully, they are learning to do the same.

Your life needs to be open. That doesn't mean you have to wear a T-shirt that says, "I have issues." It does mean, however, that within your church, or book club, or some other forum in which you are associated with other young couples or women, you need to become transparent. Hey, you may be the first, but you certainly will not be the last. Ask the Lord to guide you as you start the trend. You have no idea to whom you may minister and who may reciprocally minister to you. Allow God to use you in the places that you are most fearful of being exposed. Ladies, we have to tear down these walls that the enemy has built. We are so blinded with pride in our homes, families, cars, positions and titles that we keep helping him build, brick by brick. Share with one another from your experiences; be open and honest with one another. These walls that the enemy has built are far from transparent, so there's no other way around them other than to simply tear them down. I have started by exposing myself and that is one brick. Now it is your turn.

The Emotional Roller Coaster

I hate those days when I don't want to get out of bed. I'm not sleepy, and I hear my alarm clock blasting, but I just don't want to face the day. I call those my frustration days. It's a peculiar challenge because I often find myself, once again, faced with my own questions regarding my self-worth. I know you have questioned yours also at some point in your life, perhaps today. Some women have even birthed babies just to give their life value or purpose. We are much more than that and I have to believe that, as I have not yet produced children. Yet, it is hard to find your worth on a frustration day. My train of thought usually goes something like the following:

> AM I OPERATING IN THE PLANS THAT YOU HAVE FOR ME LORD? OR ARE THOSE THE PLANS THAT MY FAMILY HAS FOR ME, OR THE PLANS THAT I THINK PEOPLE EXPECT OF ME? IS WHAT I AM DOING TODAY CONTRIBUTING TO WHAT YOU WANT ME TO DO LORD?

Frustration is often the result of our impatience with God, and it can sometimes be a by-product when we are not in accordance with the Lord's plans. Thus we have to learn how to walk away from our plans if they do not fall in line with the will of God. Yet to do so, we have to understand what that will is. "'*For I know the plans I have for you*' declares the Lord, '*plans to prosper you and not to harm you, plans to give you hope and a future*'" *Jeremiah 29:11, NIV*. I have read that scripture and heard that word taught thousands of times, but I am often left screaming to God: "Well, if you know them, would you mind sharing them with me so I can quit wasting time?" This little episode usually takes place on one of those frustration days that we all experience whether you are married, single, divorced or separated. We all get discouraged with our lives or we face days where we feel rejection, self-pity, humiliation or loneliness. For some reason, it is on those days that I feel as though I have the liberty to complain and make demands upon the Lord to reveal all of His plans for my life just so that I can feel better and rise out of the bed for the day. Well, God does not work that way. He is not going to jump at my every command. Now, my earthly father - that may be a slightly different story. I have been truly blessed with a great dad. He did and still does everything he can to shower me with love and affection and to help meet my needs. Yet God, our supreme dad, does not operate on our time. He does not operate according to what we beg of Him. He operates on His time, and we just have to trust that He operates with our best interests at heart.

The bottom line is that you will have frustrating days. You are not going to know all of the plans and every single move to make, or every direction to turn. You have to learn to trust the Holy Spirit that is speaking to you in your heart when making decisions or simply when trying to get out of bed. Don't make choices based on emotions and on a whim, such as leaving a job because your boss made you angry and suddenly, *you hear the Lord calling you to another job*. That is usually more you than it is God. While it may be difficult to sit among many gifted people at your job or in your church as you wonder about your gifts and talents and when or how they will be used, you just cannot move to another city or change churches every time you are in a place where you are feeling frustrated or you simply do not fit in. It may be hard to walk in fear that if you let people get close enough, they will see that you are not everything they thought you were, or that you even thought you were. It may be hard to smile on the outside when you arrive at your destination while all morning or afternoon you have been crying. It is hard, but the Word of the Lord says that *"he will turn your mourning into dancing and your sorrow into joy"* See Psalm 30:11, KJV.

Learn to trust the Lord. He will lead you, not from disappointment to disappointment, but from faith to faith. Trust that He always has your best interests at heart. Trust that for every failure, there is actually a lesson learned. That for every "no," there is the greater "yes" to come. *"Trust in the Lord with all of your heart and lean not to your own understanding. In all your ways acknowledge him, and he shall direct your paths"* Proverbs 3:5–6, KJV. Acknowledge Him first thing in the morning. Let's stop waking up dreading the day, and let's wake up giving Him glory and honor and thanksgiving. *"This is the day that the Lord has made, let us rejoice and be glad in it"* Psalm 118:24, KJV. Let that be true every day. If you learn to rejoice in the tribulations, the sufferings and the tears, you will certainly rejoice in the celebrations and the victories. God is a mighty fortress in the time of trouble so learn to lean on your fortress, and continue to push forward. *See Jeremiah 16:19.*

It is okay to have frustrating days. We all take a ride on that emotional roller coaster in our lives. We question our worth, our purpose and our plans. It is okay to cry through those days as you try to push through them - just learn as you push forward. Do something other than wallow in self-pity, wondering why it seems the world is against you. There is no surprise to that, because the world is against you. Yet as you read, study, and meditate on the Word of God, you will learn that as the righteousness in Christ Jesus, you are no longer a part of that world. The demonic forces within this world are not on your side, but *"if God is for us, than who can be against us?" Romans 8:31, NIV. "Greater is he that is in you, than he that is in the world" 1 John 4:4, NIV. "We are more than conquerors through Jesus Christ who loves us!" Romans 8:37, KJV.*

As for these minuscule, frustrating days, we are just passing through. As I pass through, I am just making sure to document what I feel and what I read for those who will pass through behind me. I have learned to do something other than wallow in my tears. I have learned to push through my discouraging days. Follow me, ladies, as you pass through your valleys and low places. Follow me to a place of peace. While I once thought having peace meant that nothing bothered you or you were never upset, I have since learned that you can have peace even in the midst of your storms in life. You can have peace even on a frustrating day, so even though I may cry at times, I am at peace.

I equate those frustrating days with driving through a tumultuous rainstorm. As the rain pounds onto your car windshield, your visibility diminishes to what lies ahead. Although you cannot see as well as you would like to, you cannot and you do not stop driving because there is somewhere that you need to be. So what do you do? You turn on the windshield wipers, slow down your speed, and keep driving. That is exactly what you have to do in the midst of your tears on those frustrating days. Don't stop driving. There is someplace that God is calling you, but in order to get there you will have to drive through the rain. Turn on your wipers ladies, and keep driving. *"Even though I walk through the valley of the shadow of death, I will fear no evil, for you are with me; your rod and your staff, they comfort me" Psalm 23: 4, NIV*

No Mistakes with God

I babysit for my niece and nephew quite often and I usually check in on them as they sleep. One evening I looked in
on my niece and I was just enamored with her. Although a few
short hours before she was running wild throughout the house,
as she rested, I watched her glowing in peace and innocence.
One night, she and I took in a good episode of *Berenstain Bears*
before I read her a story and tucked her in for the night. As she
watched those crazy bears trying to do something for their bear
community, I watched her. I prayed over her life as I realized
that she represents the next generation of up-and-coming "thirtysomethings." I wonder how different her life is going to be
from mine.

Her generation will start the cycle over again of marrying as
young virgins. I came to this realization as I recently attended a
wedding of a young couple who also married as virgins. It is definitely a new season. There is a shift taking place in which more
and more young people are choosing to live holy and to remain
virgins until marriage. Many of you read that sentence and do
not believe it, but we have to stop believing what we think we see
and start confessing the Word of God. Somehow we lost that.
We have to stop talking about how bad things are around us and
start professing the Lord's authority. What I see are many young
couples, both college students and younger, finding Christian
mates. Growing up, I didn't know many young couples that

were making a decision to date, but to also live holy before the Lord. I wonder how different my life would be if I had.

As I watch my niece, I want so much more for her, and she will get it. I pray that she will never know the pain I have felt, or the loneliness, the bitterness, the envy, or the insecurities that I have suffered. These are all feelings that the enemy forced on me when he stole my purity. However, the one thing he did not count on is that I would rise up again and redirect all of that pain into what I write to you today. Now, no matter what punches he throws at me, I know that my Redeemer lives, and because He lives, I live. As for me, I choose to live in peace, purity, prosperity, health and happiness. I have traded in my sorrows and those years of torture. I have traded them in for the joy of the Lord because I have been washed by the blood of the Lamb and I am once again pure. So are you.

Choices Are Not Mistakes

Wherever you are in life, there is an opportunity in front of you. Don't worry, you haven't missed it. We often waste so much time fixating on lost opportunities and "should haves." Let's stop dwelling on what we think is lost. Let's not focus on the things we wish we had or had not done. "Why did I do that?" or "Why didn't I just _____?" You fill in your blank. I have plenty of blanks that I continue to beat myself up about. Take a moment and notice that I did not use the word *mistakes*. In hindsight, I'm not sure that they were mistakes. I didn't make a mistake; I made a choice. Learn to accept the *choices* that you have made and from now on, refer to them as choices, not mistakes.

I often wonder whether I would change my path in life if I could. I am honestly not sure that I would. We often think things would have been easier or better for us if only we had not made some of the choices we had. The truth is that you really do not and cannot know that. We can only daydream and imagine what life might have been, but even that is a very uncertain "might." What you can know is that for every choice that you may have made that was outside the will of God, you can make one that is totally within His will to correct it. The Lord finds a way to weave every bad choice into His ultimate plan for your life. His will shall be done in your life; it is just a lot easier if we submit to it by obedience rather than sacrifice. *"And we know that in all things God works for the good of those who love him, who have been called according to his purpose" Romans 8:28, NIV.*

Stop looking back in your life. Make this your year of exodus from your past. Read the story throughout Exodus and Numbers and how Moses led the children of Israel out of Egypt. God was trying to lead them into the Promised Land of Canaan, but their biggest hindrance was themselves. They continuously complained and kept looking back to what their life was like in Egypt. They were slaves in Egypt! Yet, rather than push forward to a promise of a better life ahead of them, they longed for the former days of slavery. We are often the biggest obstacles in our own lives. God has led you out of a situation, out of a city, and out of a relationship with a promise to carry you into a better land. Yet, you have to keep looking forward and not at what you left behind. Trade in the sorrows and the choices of the past for the joy of the Lord that is ahead of you. Allow the Lord to come into your life, cleanse you and purify you again.

Pray with me: *Forgive me, Lord for every time that I have looked back and said perhaps I was better off. Lord, I know that my latter days are destined to be greater than my past days. I will look forward and no longer behind me. I am on my way to my destiny in you, Christ Jesus. Amen.*

Now, the hardest part is what I am going to say next: Learn to forgive yourself. Let me say that once again. We have to learn to forgive ourselves. It is much easier to believe that God forgives us. The Word promises that *"if we confess our sins, he is faithful and just and will forgive us our sins and purify us from all unrighteousness" 1 John 1:9, NIV*. If God reigns supreme, and in His sovereignty He has forgiven you, can't you forgive yourself? Sure, you can talk the talk about how much you love yourself, and how happy you are, but who are you really convincing when you continue to beat yourself up over past choices? I know personally how hard it is to forgive oneself. Some days I want to kick myself for the stupid things I've done, but I can't. Well, I know now that my mistakes weren't mistakes at all; they were choices. Choices that I have definitely learned from, but they are in the past and there is nothing I can do about them. I had to forgive myself. So do you. *"Not that I have already obtained all this or have already been made perfect, but I press on to take hold of that which Christ Jesus took hold of me. I do not consider myself yet to have taken hold of it. But one thing I do: Forgetting what is behind and straining toward what is ahead, I press on toward the goal to win the prize for which God has called me heavenward in Christ Jesus" Philippians 3:12–14, NIV.*

RESTORATION COMETH

There are no mistakes and nothing is ever lost under God's authority. He is all-powerful, all-knowing and all-seeing. If you think something is lost, He knows where it is. We often think we've lost something or missed out on something because of some bad choice that we haven't forgiven ourselves for. The truth is that it is never really lost; the devil just stole it. For example, I always tend to forget where I park my car when I go into the shopping mall or the grocery store. Yes, I am the person wandering the parking lot aisle pretending to look for my keys or talk on my cell phone, but what I'm actually doing is looking for my car. I know that eventually I'm going to find it. But if you're the person who never forgets where you parked and you came outside to discover that your car was gone, you wouldn't say, "I lost my car." You would say, "Somebody stole my car and I have to find it!" That's what we need to start saying for *all* of our stuff. The enemy stole our stuff and we are coming to find it! We want it all back: our visions and dreams, our families, our health, our wealth and our purity! We want every prophetic word that has been spoken over our lives! Take authority in your life and take back everything the enemy stole from you!

God will restore everything that we think we have ever lost, including time. If time runs out, He will make more time. He creates time because He is time! Stretch your mind to the possibility that perhaps thirty, thirty–four, thirty-seven or thirty-nine is not the end of time for you. Remove every limitation from God because it is not over for you. Your time did not run out. You are not forgotten, you are not abandoned, and there are no mistakes with God. Open up your mind to believe that restoration cometh. *"And I will restore to you the years that the locust hath eaten . . ." Joel 2:25, KJV.*

In the Meantime

As of this year, there at least fifteen weddings that I have participated in as either a hostess, or as the ever-dreadful bridesmaid. After I had accumulated a plethora of wedding dresses, I finally had to create new positions for myself at weddings. I became the wedding coordinator, the bride's personal assistant, and sometimes (when I was lucky) just the guest. It doesn't matter what my title has been; I have never been the bride.

How did I end up in so many weddings? Well, I took an extended amount of time in finishing my undergraduate degree. Thus, by the time I finished, I had accumulated an entire new age group of friends. These friends would also go through the wedding stage just two years behind my first group of friends. What a mess I got myself into! You can't say no to your friends, can you? Well, I had to start. Your true friends will understand, or at least will say they understand. Your only hope is that they also become engulfed in the bridesmaid cycle so they begin to understand your position. I finally just stopped going to weddings altogether, but that didn't help much, either. It's not my friend's fault that she's getting married before me. Actually, it's not a "fault" at all. It's life - the life that God has designed for me.

I have actually learned to laugh about it. It is really quite hilarious because you sit back and watch your friends choose *your* wedding colors, *your* dress style and *your* shoes (but rarely the man you would have chosen). Then the years move forward and you watch again as your friends choose the name you were saving for *your* baby - the name of your daughter, the name of your son. What can you do? You can't get angry with your friends because it's not as if you're pregnant or married. For goodness sake, you may not even be dating! So what do you do? You find a way to not whine or cry about it. There is nothing you can do. You cannot speed up your process. You cannot force something to happen. I know that at times it can be very troublesome. I hate saying it myself, yet it is what it is - time and patience.

In the meantime, don't waste time. God has designed your life accordingly and there is something for you to discover now. Do something with yourself. Develop a skill, begin a hobby or volunteer. Take a class or go back to school. Don't sit on the shelf and decide to just stay in that same place waiting for your Prince Charming to come. Prince Charming may not be coming for a long time. Further, when you do meet him, it's very likely that you won't recognize him as a prince. Your best bet is to stay focused on the plans that God has for your life. One caveat: Do not do something just for the sake of doing it. Do something that is within the will of God. Do something that can be used to better His Kingdom. If you find something you love to do or that comes naturally for you, the chances are strong that it is within the will of God. Stop envying those who have discovered fascinating hobbies or careers that they love and start seeking your own. For me, I realized that the thoughts I have been working out in my head for years, and the discussions I have had over the years with my friends, needed to be written down. Once I began to write, I realized that I loved it. Since I began this endeavor, I crave it. I often cannot wait for the evening to come, which is when I would usually crawl into bed and watch some mindless show to entertain myself. Now I long for that time because I cannot wait to jump on my computer to jot my thoughts down.

Once God moves in your life He just moves, and there is nothing you can do about it. Interestingly enough, we hate that there is nothing that we can do about our circumstances when it seems like there is nothing out there for us. In other words, when we are in the "meantime." Yet once God's blessings start overflowing in our lives, we love that there is nothing that we can do about it. So again I say just be patient and step out in faith and into God, seeking only His plans for your life. When it is God, you will know it is God.

DREAM AGAIN

In the meantime, dream again. I have dreamed so many other things in my lifetime that I have actually achieved that I have to continue to dream bigger and better. Do not be afraid to dream big and believe God again and again in your life! Reflect on a word that you have received from the Lord about your life and your dreams. That word has not died and it shall not return to the Lord void. *"So is my word that goes out from my mouth: It will not return to me empty, but will accomplish what I desire and achieve the purpose for which I sent it" Isaiah 55:11, NIV.*

Just note that as you begin to dream again, some of the dreams and visions the Lord gives to you are not for sharing. It is not that everyone will not be supportive; it is that *someone* will not be supportive. I often struggle in this area, because I can't hold water! I am guilty of always needing to tell someone something. It is difficult to keep quiet sometimes because it is so natural to get excited when you feel as though the Lord has spoken to you. You want to run and tell your family, your pastor and your friends that you have heard something from the Lord. Yes, you know who you are; every time He gives you the slightest bit of insight into your purpose, you have to run up and down the aisles of the church, jumping over chairs, telling everyone! Yet, the Lord desires intimacy with you. Intimacy often involves quietness and literally keeping a secret with the Lord. So in the meantime, work on that relationship with Him. Think about it. If you have secrets with some of your closest friends, why not have secrets with God? You trust Him, right? He wants to trust you in the same way. He wants to give you more dreams and more visions, but if you are a big-mouth, He cannot and will not trust you.

Let's try something different this time; let's try to write down what the Lord reveals to you instead of telling everyone. Write it all down, ladies: every dream, every desire and every disappointment. Write it down. Habakkuk says to *"write down the revelation and make it plain on tablets so that a herald may run with it. For the revelation awaits an appointed time; it speaks of the end and will not prove false. Though it linger, wait for it; it will certainly come and will not delay"* Habakkuk 2:2–3, NIV.

Read that passage again and meditate on it. In the meantime, write down the revelations that God gives to you; write down those dreams that you have. As you are writing, be as creative as you can and enlarge your vision as wide as you can. Write it down, even if it sounds silly or impossible. Dream as big as you can, and stretch your faith to see the impossible for your life. Increase your faith as you write and dream for your life. For as high as you can dream for yourself, God's plans are even bigger. *"For my thoughts are not your thoughts, neither are your ways my ways. As the heavens are higher than the earth, so are my ways higher than your ways and my thoughts than your thoughts"* Isaiah 55:8–10, NIV.

The Television Downfall

I told myself that as I was writing, I would not take phone calls, watch television or allow any other interruptions. I have to tell you that the truth of the matter is this: When you are single and your phone rings, you answer it. I have gone too many days with "you have no messages" as my evening companion. But let's consider *what* we are watching and *who* we allow to speak in our lives. For example, we watch *Girlfriends, Sex in the City, Desperate Housewives, and The Fabulous Life of . . .* (some celebrity), and then we wonder why our thoughts are filled with loneliness, sex, masturbation, jealousy and greed. We want what those sitcoms and "not-so-reality" programs promise us we can have. They solve all of their problems in twenty-two minutes or less, so why can't we? We think, "I am living a more Christian life than they are, so why isn't God blessing me with what they have?" Well, first, let's get this straight God is not necessarily blessing them, we are. We bless them by continuing to eat what they are feeding us. We jump on the bandwagon of every new neo-soul artist that comes along because we like the smooth vibes and we buy into their "spirituality." It is time to get serious about the Lord. Stop looking to man (meaning the world) for solutions to your queries. The Word says, *"Blessed is the man who does not walk in the counsel of the wicked . . . but his delight is in the law of the Lord, and on his law he meditates day and night. He is like a tree planted by streams of water, which yields its fruit in season and whose leaf does not wither. Whatever he does prospers" Psalm 1:1–3, NIV.*

Turn off the television, the computer, and the iPod, and tune into the Word of God. Learn it for the first time or learn it all over again like a child. Go back and learn the stories of the Old Testament. Read them again for the first time and see how He directs your life. Read how God spoke to Abram, changed his name, and ordered him to another land. God may be ordering some of you to another place, perhaps for a professional change, a spiritual revival or even for a mate. The answer to some of your present-day dilemmas is in the Word, but you keep missing it because you wake up and you seek what the world provides for you. You do not seek His Word.

We are too caught up in the superficial world of television. It may even be time to shut off some of the television evangelists that we have learned to love. We get quite accustomed to someone else's version of the Bible. That is not enough. We have to learn the scriptures for ourselves, so stop relying on someone else to feed you the Word. When your back is against the wall, you need to have the Word of God written on the tablet of your heart. Many of the scriptures I have used in this book have come loosely from memory. I did not stop to search the Bible so that I could sound spiritual. I just know them. I know them because I have needed to know them in order to apply them to my life over the last few years. That did not happen overnight. I decided that I truly wanted to learn the Word, so I committed time to it. You have to learn the Word of God first so you can learn to believe it. You have to. It is the Word that gives us life and hope, wisdom and guidance. Read it, learn it, memorize it and believe it. If you're feeling convicted as you read this, you're likely not alone. I have also kicked myself for time wasted. There are so many hours that I could have turned off the television to write, read or study the Word, but that time is gone. I can never get complacent with what little knowledge I have, and neither can you. I need to read more and learn more, so I can grow more. I have only learned enough to get me to where I am now and I cannot go any further until I learn more.

Pray with me: *Lord, I want to grow and I want to be used by you. I know that in order to do this, I have to submit and commit my ways to you. So today, Lord, I will stop and take time in your Word.*

Submit to Whom?

Submission. Now that's a word you either love or hate. We often equate that word with being married, but submission begins long before you walk into a marriage covenant. Submission is tantamount with humility because it often takes humility to truly submit to anyone but yourself. Most of us have a hard time submitting to the Lord, let alone to others. If you're not sure what submission is or to whom you should submit, read carefully. Submission is not just for married people. Submission is for anyone who sits in someone else's church, job, theatrical production, school or whatever - it is for everyone.

One of the most profound and intriguing stories of submission in the Bible is the story of Sarai and her maidservant Hagar. Unwisely, Sarai ordered her husband Abram into the loving arms of Hagar because Sarai was unable to give him a child. Although the Lord had promised Sarai that she would bear children, she became impatient and took matters into her own hands. Hagar became pregnant with the child that Sarai could not have. Eventually, Sarai became increasingly jealous and ultimately ordered Hagar out of their city. Hagar obediently fled, but while in exile she was met by an angel of the Lord. *See Genesis 16.*

Now, imagine being Hagar. She really didn't do anything wrong; she just followed orders as a maidservant was supposed to do. Yet for her obedience, she was paid with embarrassment, humiliation and disgrace. She was forced away from her home in shame, only to be met by this angel instructing her to return to Sarai's home. The angel's message to her was to return regardless of the circumstances and to submit once again to Sarai's authority. I can just imagine Hagar thinking, "Are you crazy? That woman is nuts!" Yet, Hagar was obedient. She returned and ultimately she was blessed for submitting once again.

For women, it is often quite challenging to submit to another woman, especially within the church. Why is it so hard to submit to another woman? We usually find it difficult because we're so accustomed to competing with one another. However, isn't that what we do daily on our jobs or in school? Don't we submit to that person who exceeds us in credentials or longevity at a job? If we submit daily to these people who are often unsaved, why is it so difficult to find a woman in the church that we can submit to and be accountable to? Is it that you have more education than she does? Is it that you are not impressed with her style of dress, hair or makeup? I'm not talking about a role model; I'm talking about someone who can "call you" on your faults, in love. I'm talking about a person whom you know to seek the face of the Lord on a regular basis, thus you can listen and take heed. We all need that person or persons in our lives.

We are too sensitive as Christian women, especially when it comes to other women. It's almost as if no one can *tell us* anything. We tend to carry these "no-nonsense" attitudes around like badges of honor. We have these Claire Huxtable complexes in which every spoken word must flow off our tongues in some legalistic poetic rhythm as if we are scolding Elvin for making yet another chauvinistic remark. Listen, the Cosbys were over in the early nineties, and although you can catch the reruns twenty times a day, you're not on television and no one is impressed by your quick and witty responses. Submit. She must be saved and led by the Holy Spirit. How will you know her? You will know her by her fruit. Her fruit is her lifestyle, and the products thereof. Look for the fruit of the Spirit to be manifest in her life: love, joy, peace, patience, kindness, goodness, faithfulness, gentleness and self-control. *See Galatians 5:22.* Look for someone with good fruit, and submit. *"Likewise, every good tree bears good fruit, but a bad tree bears bad fruit. A good tree cannot bear bad fruit, and a bad tree cannot bear good fruit. Every tree that does not bear good fruit is cut down and thrown into the fire. Thus, by their fruit you will recognize them"* Matthew 7: 17–20, NIV.

All Things Through Jesus Christ

Rejoice! Do you know that you have dominion over this earth? God gave Adam and Eve authority over every living thing on this earth when He created them. *See Genesis 1:28.* As their descendants, we have that same authority and dominion. Understanding and believing this principle is vital for your life's journey. It is important in the little things as well as the big things in our lives. For example, when you have those "I don't want to get out of bed days," you can be confident in knowing that whatever you face, through Jesus Christ, you have authority. *"I can do all things through Jesus Christ who strengthens me" Philippians 4:13, KJV.* I know we've all heard this same scripture repeated over and over again, so why should it make any difference to you now? We all know it; even unsaved people know that scripture. We have all either heard or recited it at some beauty pageant, swim meet, basketball game, church picnic, children's play, car wash . . . you name it, we have used it. We have allowed the "world" to take what is one of the most important scriptures in the Bible, and neutralize it to the point that it is diluted to an empty mantra.

Lord, please forgive us for diluting your Word and using it carelessly and please refresh us and restore our hearts and minds to receive that word from you as fresh dew in the morning. Amen.

Okay, now that we're all rejuvenated for the Word, let's dissect that scripture as if it were the first time we were hearing it:

I: This means you and me ladies, no matter what your situation is right now. If you are living with a man who is not your husband (even if you are engaged), this includes you. If you have never allowed the Lord into your life, this means you. If you have been saved all of your life, this means you. If you struggle with fear or insecurities, this means you. It means all of us.

CAN DO: This is more profound than we often interpret it to be. We often read this to say, "I can if I want to," but I choose to read this as saying "I must do." Think about it - we're going to have to do something in our lives. We're not going to sit on our couches every day and watch television from sunup to sundown (and if that is you, then get your behind up and go to work for the Kingdom)! You have to do something every day, and the Word of God says to commit everything you do to the Lord. *See Psalm 37:5*. So it is not just that you "can," because we already know that we "can." When thinking about your purpose in the Kingdom of God, it is not a "can," it is a "must."

ALL THINGS: This is the part that you may not like. Sometimes we go after the things that *we* want instead of the things that God wants for us. Some of us do this, knowing that it is not God's plan for our lives, but we still choose to make it our plan. This part of the scripture is likely the reason the scripture has been reduced to empty chatter in the lives of Christians. We use it so casually for everything we think we want. But if it is not in the will of God, it is not for you to do, or even attempt to do. We sometimes try to twist that reasoning and apply it to something that perhaps we do not want to do, although we know God is calling us. We often stretch and interpret the Word to fit our life pattern instead of stretching ourselves to fit within the pattern of the Word. This means "all things" that are within the will of God.

THROUGH JESUS CHRIST: You cannot do anything *through* Christ if He does not live in you. This means that you must be saved. To receive from Him, He must live in your hearts, minds and souls. Ladies, you cannot walk this journey on your own. Even if you are married, engaged or in a serious relationship, you will always need Christ as your first love. Make room in your heart for Him. If you want to receive His strength, His love, His mercy and His grace, you must be saved. For those of you who do not know, salvation is not coming to church every week, or being the hardest-working deacon in the pews. Salvation is a voluntary confession with your mouth and a simple belief in your heart. If you believe in your heart that Christ is the Son of God and that He died on the cross for your sins, you can be saved by simply repeating the next few lines aloud:

Lord, I am a sinner. I believe that you sent your son Jesus Christ to die on the cross for my sins, and I believe that he rose again and he is Lord. I now ask for you, Jesus, to forgive me of my sins and to cleanse me from all unrighteousness. I invite you Lord Jesus to come and live in my heart, forever. From this day forward, I will live for you and I will never be the same again. Amen.

Drum roll please . . . you are now saved! You are restored, rejuvenated, refreshed, purified and righteous! People have trouble believing that it is just that simple, but it is and His Word proves it:

If you confess with your mouth, "Jesus is Lord," and believe in your heart that God raised him from the dead, you will be saved. For it is with your heart that you believe and are justified, and it is with your mouth that you confess and are saved . . . Everyone who calls on the name of the Lord will be saved.
Romans 10: 9–10, 13, NIV.

If you remember a few chapters back, I told you how conniving the devil is. Do not be surprised if he is whispering to you right now that you cannot be saved: "Remember what you did last night, or even this morning? Remember that abortion or sleeping with that married man?" That's how he tries to kill us softly, but when he starts speaking to you, allow that "believe in your heart" part of the prayer to kick in. You must believe in your salvation. It is that simple. You have authority over the devil, so if he is whispering to you right now, say, "Devil, the Lord has given me authority over you and I command you to shut up!" See, now that Jesus is in your life, you have more power than you could have ever imagined.

WHO STRENGTHENS ME: Now this is where the power comes in. Feel God's love in your heart because His love is your source of power. Acknowledge how much He loves you and allow Him to love you. Draw upon His love, mercy and protection as your source of power. He is all-powerful and all-loving. He is who He says He is - God Almighty. *See Genesis 17*. I often think of Him as a superhero with every imaginable type of power. He can stop or start tumultuous storms. He can create fire in a rain shower and He can do anything because He controls the entire universe. *"The earth is the Lord's, and everything in it, the world, and all who live in it; for he founded it upon the seas and established it upon the waters" Psalm 24:1–2, NIV.*

Let's read that scripture again: *"I can do all things through Jesus Christ who strengthens me" Philippians 4:13*. I imagine that you will never read it the same way again.

I Know the Plans I Have for You

You are destined for greatness. Do you believe that? If your answer was an emphatic "yes," praise God and walk into that destiny. For those of you who may have read right through that first line without really pondering it or thinking of its application to you, pay close attention to the next few lines. *You are destined for greatness. You are destined for greatness. You are destined for greatness.* Say it aloud daily. Say it so much that it resonates in your ears even when you are not saying it. First say it, then begin believing it. Saying it aloud makes it available to you to receive. Believing it makes it available for you to become. *You are destined for greatness.*

Now let's discuss what greatness really is. The easiest way is to determine what it is not. Greatness is not success according to western civilization's standards. It appears to be, but that's because we idolize and place those who have achieved a certain level of success on a pedestal. Unfortunately, this type of success is worthless if you are not within the will of God. While your tangible possessions and your physical body may prosper, your soul does not. *"What good will it be for a man if he gains the whole world, yet forfeits his soul?" Matthew 16:26, NIV.* You do not want to give up your soul and eternity with God in order to achieve that type of worldly success.

Yet there is a level of greatness in God that he wants us all to reach. You can reach this level by understanding your purpose, walking in your purpose, and maximizing your purpose. It is not good enough to casually walk into our purpose; God wants us to take full advantage of it. This means to remove all limitations from yourself and, more importantly, from God.

UNDERSTANDING PURPOSE

Millions of people have read Rick Warren's *The Purpose Driven Life* and we understand that life is not solely about our happiness. Our main goal should be to seek after the plans and desires that God has for us and happiness is often a by-product or bonus of seeking those plans. Finding your purpose will not likely be achieved by constantly running to prophets, pastors and ministers, searching for someone to speak to your life and explain it to you. Your purpose is laid out for you and found in the Word of God, thus we have to know the Word, understand it, learn it and hide it in our hearts. The psalmist says *"I have hidden your word in my heart that I might not sin against you" Psalm 119:11, NIV*. We sin against the Lord by seeking our will instead of His will for our lives.

How do we seek His will? We have to discipline and train ourselves to read and study the Word of God. I admit I too have been lazy in this area. (No wonder it has taken me so long to start realizing my purpose!) Laziness and excuses will keep you in the dark about the Lord's plans for your life. Take the time to read. There are books upon books telling you how to read the Word, but the simplest method is to just start from the beginning. I decided to invest more than twenty dollars and I purchased a Life Application Bible. It does exactly that–applies the Bible to your life. It has pages of footnotes describing the history and background of each chapter to help you understand the context of the scriptures. It also modernizes the scriptures making them relevant to your present day situation reminding you that the Bible is not just history, it is your present and future.

The Word can be overwhelming when taken as a whole, so take it little by little, and day by day. Turn off the television at night so you can go to bed and get up a little earlier each morning. Start off small if you need, with just ten to fifteen minutes of your time spent reading the Word, then gradually increase as you can. Ask the Lord to reveal His plan for your life as you read, then actually read! You can read for enjoyment, because we all know the Bible is filled with radical and miraculous stories. Yet also read for direction, asking the Lord to guide you and open your ears to hear from Him as you read. Read for wisdom and to find intimacy with God. You may find direction for your current situation in a few lines or chapters, or you may not hear anything from the Lord until you have read for days. Just read, and as scriptures begin to jump out at you and minister to you, memorize them. That is *hiding the Word in your heart* as the psalmist did. As the Lord speaks to you, write down the words that come to your heart and the scriptures that correspond. These are revelations from the Lord, and Habakkuk instructs us to write the revelation down. *See Habakkuk 2.*

Your story may parallel that of Noah, Isaiah, Timothy or Paul. See yourself as God speaks to Abraham and tells him to walk through the land that He had provided for him. Then go out and find the land that the Lord has for you. Keep reading. Early on, you will read how the wives of our forefathers, Sarah, Rebecca and Rachel, all had trouble bearing children. Yet the Lord miraculously produced children in each of their wombs. You may be well beyond the years of childbearing, according to the timetable of this earth, but the same miracles the Lord provided for them are available for you if you trust in the Lord.

As you read, the Lord will begin to reveal things to you about your life. As this happens, begin to walk into what the Lord says to you. Listen to the Lord, but do not move with haste. I'm often guilty of that myself. I want things done quickly because I'm a part of the microwave generation. "Do it quickly

Lord, and hurry it up!" Well, the Lord does not operate according to the buttons we push, so we just have to be patient, diligent and disciplined.

STEP INTO GOD

What else is the Lord saying to you? You will find it as you read and begin to understand your purpose. This may be your year to start building, dreaming and planning. While this may not be your immediate year of execution, it could certainly be your year to start the preparations. What God has for you is for you. Do you realize how many different visions those scriptures have inspired? Do you think all of the visions are gone and used up? Never! We just have to step out in faith and grab onto the visions and dreams the Lord gives to us. We can't sit and wait for something to fall into our laps.

Once again, as I write to you, I am writing to myself. I have never thought of myself as an entrepreneurial type. I have often thought that things would just happen for me or that I would just walk into something. Sorry, Charlie, but things usually don't work that way. God can only meet you where you are willing to go. That's why we call it a step of faith. It's not faith stepping toward you - it's you stepping toward faith. We don't wake up one day with tremendous faith. Each of us is either taking steps toward faith or away from faith every day of our lives. Which direction are you heading? *"Now faith is being sure of what we hope for and certain of what we do not see . . . And without faith it is impossible to please God, because anyone who comes to him must believe that he exists and that he rewards those who earnestly seek him" Hebrews 11:1, 6, NIV.*

Most of us have experienced a brush with death at some point in our lives. For me, it was a traumatic near-miss car accident. I have been in a couple of those scenarios where I might have been seriously injured, perhaps even killed, but this particular one was different. Perhaps it was different because I was alone in the car this time. Or perhaps it felt different because I had been in a recent struggle with God's plan for my life. It was just different. I was coming out of the grocery store parking lot and I approached the traffic light. I stopped, as my light was red, and I started to look for something tucked away in the armrest. Apparently the light turned green but I hadn't noticed. No one was behind me to honk, and I was not looking. When I did look up, I noticed it was my turn to go. I began to proceed into the intersection as my radio was blasting Israel Houghton's "Nothing Can Stop the Favor of the Lord," and I was singing along with him. It happened in a millisecond. I glanced to the left and saw a large, white car speeding in my direction and I slammed on my brakes. In that split second I looked to the light to make sure that I had seen it correctly, and it was in fact green (although that would not have mattered if I had died). The car sped right through the intersection, pausing only briefly after passing through. I don't think the driver saw the red light at all. I sat in the intersection for a few more seconds as the tears began to stream down my face. My heart was racing and my head was pounding. Even while writing this I cannot hold back the tears because of how afraid I was at that moment. What I remember best was how clear the Lord's word was immediately after I hit my brakes. I heard the word "purpose." I didn't hear an audible voice; I just heard it in my head. It was as if I was saying it in my head to myself. Then I realized that it was the Lord speaking to me.

What does this mean for you? I believe that near-death experience happened to me, not only so the Lord could remind me that He has a plan for my life, but so I could share that with you and remind you of your experiences. Many of us should be dead for one reason or another, but we are not. It's not because the devil has not tried to kill us. (Remember that he comes only to kill, steal and destroy.) You are still alive because God has a plan for your life. He has spared you and protected you for *His* will, not yours. You owe Him your life, so surrender it to Him, and recognize Him as sovereign in your life. You have to trust that your life is in fact a purpose-driven life. *"Trust in the Lord with all your heart and lean not on your own understanding; in all your ways acknowledge him and he will make your paths straight"* *Proverbs 3:5–6, NIV.* Do not give up on God and do not let the enemy tell you that you have nothing to give and thus you are worthless. Stop looking all around to find your worth; your worth is found in the blood of the Lamb Jesus. You are worth living, so live! Thank Him right now for your life and surrender your plans into His plans again.

God has a plan for your life. It may not seem like it today, and you may not feel as though you are doing anything worthwhile. Just step out in faith and God will meet you. I must caution you that when you take this step and He meets you, fasten your seatbelt and learn how to trust Him, because once He moves, it may all happen at once. As I write this, I think back to the drive from my house in Atlanta to take the Kaplan preparatory class for the LSAT (law school admission test). Every day that I took that drive, I listened to Yolanda Adams singing "I believe that I can make it" as I prayed to God for wisdom and direction. I wasn't sure if I was doing the right thing. I left a good, stable job, to step out and try something new. I remember a particular passage in an inspirational book that read in part, God will start opening doors and making connections for you once you step out in faith. That is exactly what happened for me. I wasn't sure about applying to law school, partly due to the financial commitment. Yet, I just stepped out in faith and went through the application process. I applied to seven schools and got accepted into every school. For the icing on the cake, five of the schools offered me scholarship money! Trust me, my undergraduate grades weren't that great, so it had to be God! That experience was one of the many reminding me that all we have to do is get up every day, commit our plans to the Lord and be disciplined and open to hear from Him. Be willing to change directions, and be flexible with God. Step away from your own plans and schedule. *"If you are willing and obedient, you will eat the best from the land; but if you resist and rebel, you will be devoured by the sword" Isaiah 1:19–20, NIV.* God wants you to eat from the best of the land if you will be willing and obedient.

This is especially difficult for women because by nature, we are often planners. We will design a plan that must be enacted as scheduled, and we will stick to this plan no matter what. Yet, when it comes to the will of God, we have to learn to break away from *our* plans and *our* schedules. Don't become so focused, determined and bound by your plans that you miss something God has for you. It may be in a total different direction then what you had in mind, and it may be hard to walk away from something that is so comfortable, convenient and familiar. Don't be afraid to step out in faith and see God meet you there. I call it stepping out into God.

The best way that I can describe it is to think about when you are dressed up and leaving your home to go somewhere. You have taken your time getting dressed, your outfit is gorgeous, your hair fell right into place and your makeup is flawless. Everything is right and you are heading out on a date with a significant other, with your friends, or just by yourself. The moment you step out your door there's a feeling you get, like a rush. It's an air of confidence that surrounds you. It's as if you are the most beautiful person walking the face of the earth. That's the same feeling that I get when I step out into God. I feel like there is nothing that I cannot do. There is nothing too hard. It is almost inexplicable; you have to try it to feel it. Try it - step out into God. You will never look back.

Pray with me: *Lord, thank you that you are the creator of all things. Thank you that man's time does not control, but it is your divine order which controls our lives, our purpose and our destiny. I release my plans and schedule over to you and I am stepping out in faith to follow the plans that you have for my life. Amen.*

The World Belongs to the Disciplined

It is time to learn how to pray and seek the Kingdom of God for yourself. I was reminded of this once when I received a wedding invitation in the mail. I laughed as I opened the reception card and the couple had already checked the number "1" to indicate how many will be attending in my party. I understand that is the new trend in order to keep folks from bringing themselves, plus two of their cousins; but I could not help but laugh at that simple gesture as it applies to singleness. I laughed and thought, "What? They don't even think I can get a date? How do they know I won't meet someone by the date of the wedding? How do they know I'm not dating someone now?"

The point of my sharing this little episode with you is to emphasize that other people will likely have less faith than you that God has someone for you. Thus, you had better learn to have faith for yourself. However, this is not just about having faith for a mate, or for children. This applies to all aspects of your life. You may be slipping and sliding with a bunch of "near misses" in your life, but let me explain that you have likely been riding on the wave of your parents' and grandparents' prayers for your life.

News Flash: You can no longer rely on someone else's faith and prayers for your life. It is time for you to learn how to seek the face of the Lord for yourself.

Now is the time to discipline yourself in the Word of God.

Discipline is a practice. You don't wake up one day and just have it, you cultivate it. It's a behavior. It sets you apart from others around you. Discipline is getting up early or staying up late to accomplish some task. It is submitting yourself to something that others will not. Discipline is pushing yourself harder and further than others will or than you thought you could. Discipline builds your character and as a thank-you, your character produces more discipline. Discipline doesn't come easy; it requires sacrifice and commitment. You have to train yourself to do that which you probably do not want to do in order to be disciplined. This usually will not happen overnight.

If you have a desire to go back to school, trust me, it will not be easy. I returned to school when I was twenty-eight years old. It was difficult at times to sit in class with several bright-eyed and bushy-tailed twenty-two-year-olds. Many of them had never worked a day in their lives, yet they believed they were going to change the world. It is difficult to find some common ground with them just to survive the two to three years you commit to this endeavor. It is not easy, but it is achievable.

Law school actually starts before your first day of classes because the professors give reading assignments that you must be prepared to discuss on the first day of class. I remember crying through my first reading assignment, thinking, "What have I gotten myself into?" It was only my first assignment and I was ready to quit! It took me three hours to read one assignment and I had three other classes to read for. I remembered studying hard in pharmacy school, but that had been three years before. On that first night of reading, and for about the next month, I honestly did not think I had it in me to study that hard again. My precious Aunt, who had also attended law school and is now a judge, called and wrote me quite frequently to encourage me to keep going. I kept a card from her on my desk, where I spent countless hours reading. It read, "You can do this!" in big letters. I must have read those words thousands of times over the next few months. *I can do this. I can do this.* I told the Lord that I would not be lazy, but I could not make it through this program without Him. I woke up early to study and go to class. I turned off the television and shut off my phone. I suffered through the embarrassing days of speaking in class, often not knowing what I was talking about! I cut back on my expenses and I missed out on some birthdays, reunions, anniversaries, weddings and other special occasions. I trained myself to sit still and read, and when I wanted to go to bed, I would read some more. It was not easy. Some days were great, and some days I was literally in tears. I questioned my choice to go back to school quite frequently and I often thought about dropping out. Nevertheless, the blood of Mal Goode, my grandfather, runs through my veins. I would hear his voice saying, "The world belongs to the disciplined," so I prayed every day for strength, wisdom and discipline, and the Lord provided it day after day, semester after semester, year after year.

No matter who you are or where you are in your life right now, if you desire a change in your circumstances, it will require discipline. Your desire may be to return to school, or to start your own business. You may be praying for a job promotion or even a new job. Every move that you make toward advancement is going to require some level of discipline and sacrifice on your part. You have to train yourself in order to qualify for success in any area of your life. The world belongs to the disciplined.

We also have to apply this same level of discipline to our spiritual lives, the area in which we desperately need to succeed. The Lord requires our time, our hearts and our minds. You have to train yourself to give Him these areas every day. It is unacceptable to give to everyone else, including yourself, but not to give of yourself to the Lord every day. Discipline yourself to rise early or take a midday break to fellowship with Him. You have to make it a priority. You have to make *Him* your priority.

"I discipline my body like an athlete, training it to do what

it should. Otherwise, I fear that after preaching to others I myself might be disqualified" 1 Corinthians 9: 27, NLT.

Prophesy to Yourself

We often take matters into our own hands because God's timing is just not working for us. We run from prophet to prophet, or to palm readers, or reading multiple horoscopes in an attempt to figure out which direction we should take. If you are always looking for someone to speak into your life, when do you ever grow so that you can speak into the lives of others? *"Therefore let us leave the elementary teachings about Christ and go on to maturity . . ." Hebrews 6:1, NIV.*

I am guilty of longing for someone to prophesy over me, just to tell me if I am heading in the right direction, or to simply encourage me. That may be understandable when I truly need encouragement or when the Lord truly wants to confirm something for me. However, the Lord finally showed me that I needed to sit and listen to everyone else's prophesy until I finally got it - you have to stir up the gifts that are inside of you and learn to speak words of encouragement to yourself. *"I remind you to stir up the gift of God which is in you" 2 Timothy 1:6, KJV.* That means that if you are reading and studying the Word of God, and you are praying, you can prophesy to yourself.

You have to stop crying and begging the Lord to help and encourage you when the Word says that you can prophesy to your dry bones when you are in the valley. *See Ezekiel 37:1–10.* What does that mean? You have to speak words of encouragement to yourself daily. This is a spiritual principle that even the media moguls have tapped into. I was watching an interview with a famous rapper-turned-millionaire/entrepreneur as he talked about the power of words. Now, if this rapper has tapped into this power, then we, being filled with the Spirit of the Lord, surely ought to tap into the power of our words. Even more specifically, we ought to tap into the power of the Word of the Lord. I am reminded of this often when my load piles up to that unbearable point. My calendar is overflowing and my heart begins to feel heavy with panic. When that happens, I repeat these words: "Lord, apart from you I can do nothing." *See John 15:5.* "You have allowed me to be in this position, and I know that you will equip me with the strength, energy and clarity I need in order to perform the tasks that lie ahead." It works. My heart calms down and I feel better within minutes. Think what would happen if we learned to do that for everything. His Word says to *"cast all of your anxiety on him because he cares for you" 1 Peter 5:7, NIV.* Cast your cares out; do not carry those burdens alone when the Savior wants to lighten your load. You cannot live your life without Him. You can try, but why struggle like that? Start living a life of expectation. Wake up every morning and expect the blessings of God in your life. Wake up prophesying to yourself and singing praises to the Lord. My Bishop teaches us to make a daily confession about our lives. You can have what you say, so begin to prophesy what the Word of God says about you daily. Write out your personal prophesy, memorize it and believe it. Believe it even when you cannot believe it. Speak it, even when you do not feel like speaking it. Base it on the Word of God. Here is an example to get you started:

DAILY CONFESSION:

This is the day the Lord has made. I will rejoice and be glad in it . . . See Psalm 118:24.

Lord, I will bless you at all times; your praise shall continually be in my mouth . . . See Psalm 34.

Lord, I trust you and I delight in you. I commit everything that I do and everything that I am to you . . .
See Psalm 37.

I am not here to please myself, I am here to take up my cross and follow you . . . See Luke 9:23.

Apart from you, Lord, I can do nothing . . .
See John 15:5.

I will not be conformed by this world, but I will be transformed by renewing my mind . . . See Romans 12.

Your Word says that you have a good plan for my life, to give me a purpose and hope . . . See Jeremiah 29:11.

I know that your Word will not return void . . .
See Isaiah 55:11.

Lord, I will rise to become what you have commissioned for me. I declare, Lord not my will, but Thy will be done in my life, in my family, and in all the earth.

I can do, and I will do all things through Jesus Christ who strengthens me . . . See Philippians 4:13.

Run Your Race

When I turned thirty, I ran my first race ever in my life. I ran a 10K (6.2 miles). I use the word "ran" loosely, because I actually mean "jog." Well, actually, when I say I "jog," it was more like a slow crawl! Regardless of how fast or slow I ran the race - I ran it. For me this was quite an accomplishment, seeing as I never ran competitively in high school or college. As a matter of fact, the closest I ever came to the track team was performing the long jump in junior high! Yet, I decided to take up running a few years ago mostly to maintain my weight, but also to break the curses of my family history with heart disease. Those curses stop with me!

Initially, my intent was to focus on consistently running about two miles and that was enough to satisfy me. Then something happened when I moved to Boston - certainly a running city. I watched traffic stop for people running on the busiest streets because pedestrians seem to rule the Northeast. I watched people run in more circumstances than the post office workers—rain, sleet, snow, hail, heat, and the gloom of night. Well, after watching countless runners training even in the middle of a blizzard, and after seeing race after race come down Beacon Street and Commonwealth Avenue near my home, I got motivated to give it a shot.

If you have never entered a race, whether to run, jog or walk, I highly recommend doing so. I have affectionately been told that I tend to *spiritualize* everything, and so not to disappoint, this will be no exception. A race is like nothing else you will ever do in your life. It takes discipline and commitment. I surprised myself by finding the discipline required for the training alone. I was fortunate to have a girlfriend to train with. We began our training a couple of months building up to the race, encouraging each other as we each suffered through a couple of small injuries. Then finally, the race day arrived. Around five thousand women showed up that day for the race with nearly the same number of spectators to cheer us on. Some runners were in large groups, some were in mother-daughter teams, some were there with baby carriages, and some were alone. All were ready to go. Some had been running the race for over thirty years, while others were first-timers like me. I was nervous and my stomach was in knots. Although I had practiced and trained, I was scared that I might not be able to complete the run. My goal was to finish, regardless of the time. I didn't want to have to stop and walk at any point during the race, so I was praying that my stomach wouldn't cramp, as it often had during training. As we all gathered behind the starting line, the music was blasting to get us motivated and excited for the run. After about fifteen minutes of speeches, introductions, and organizing us into timed groups, the starting gun was fired and we were off. Although I was toward the back of the crowd, I am proud to say that I completed my first race and I never had to stop to walk for a minute! Instead, I tapped into a spiritual principle that changed my life! I set my pace and kept it the entire race, just as I had trained.

Throughout the race, hundreds of women passed me. Many of them were jogging at a pace of seven or eight-minute miles. I will admit that it was hard to watch them pass, and I often wanted to speed up to catch them. However, I knew if I tried to speed up, my stomach would cramp or I would tire quickly and I would not likely finish my race. So I just watched them, and sometimes I even cheered them on. One day I may run as fast as they do, or I may not. As for now, I like my pace.

Here comes my *spiritualization*: You have to learn to run your own race in life. I cannot tell you how many of my friends and family have "passed" me in life. Some of them ran a very fast mile. They are engaged, or married, and some of them have already had all of the children they wish to have. Many of them are well situated in their careers, or they are fully operating in the gifts that God has given to them. They have simply passed me by, but I am still in this race and I have even learned to cheer them on. I have learned over the years, after many tried and failed attempts, that I cannot pick up my pace to run any faster in my life. The one thing that is guaranteed is that I am training myself by reading and studying God's Word about my life. Thus, I know that I will finish this race. You'd better believe it - I will finish.

Run your own race, and do not try to keep pace with anyone else. You are responsible for your own race and making sure you make it to the finish line. God has so much in store for you, but you have to train yourself with discipline. Remove all hindrances from your life in order to stay in the race at the pace He has set out for you. Do not try to speed Him along, do not drop out, and do not try to change the course. Just set your pace and keep running. Run your own race. *"Therefore, since we are surrounded by such a great cloud of witnesses, let us throw off everything that hinders and the sin that so easily entangles, and let us run with perseverance the race marked out for us." Hebrews 12:1, NIV*

Be Blessed!

Don't give up on the Lord. Continue to push toward Him and seek Him today while He may be found. Stop looking behind you and stop worrying about tomorrow because tomorrow presents its own problems and worries. See Matthew 6:34. This is the day to make the decision to serve the Lord. Today is the day to stop mourning, to stop envying, and to stop worrying. Today is your day to renew and refresh yourself in the Lord. That is the beauty of the morning dew - it refreshes you and rests upon your heart to renew you every day. Open your eyes and rise out of that old self and become who God wants you to become. *"If any man be in Christ, he is a new creation. The old man is gone and behold, the new man has come" 1 Corinthians 5:7, NIV.* You are a new woman, starting today.

Thank you, Lord, for the opportunity to share with your people, thank you, Lord, for your anointing that flows through me as I write. Thank you for the discipline to write what you have given me and for a story to share. Thank you for the embarrassing moments and for the hilarious moments. Thank you, Lord, for training me and teaching me humility and sacrifice. Teach me more, Lord; it is not enough. I want to learn more, be more, see more and feel more through you.

I will never claim to have had all of the experiences of life to qualify me to write to you. I have not. Yet I have had my heart broken more than once, I have had my spirit broken more than once, and I have failed miserably at many things more than once. I have also given my life to the Lord, learned to walk faithfully, learned to face my fears, and learned to love fearlessly and openly time and time again. I have taken chances and made some very bad choices in my lifetime. I have learned to be a friend, to truly love my parents, and to truly love myself. Most importantly, I am learning to love God more than ever. I hope I have inspired you to know Him better than you ever have before.

Be disciplined. Be encouraged. Be delivered.

GOD BLESS YOU!

TATE PUBLISHING *& Enterprises*

Tate Publishing is committed to excellence in the publishing industry. Our staff of highly trained professionals, including editors, graphic designers, and marketing personnel, work together to produce the very finest books available. The company reflects the philosophy established by the founders, based on Psalms 68:11,

"THE LORD GAVE THE WORD AND GREAT WAS THE COMPANY OF THOSE WHO PUBLISHED IT."

If you would like further information, please call
1.888.361.9473
or visit our website
www.tatepublishing.com

TATE PUBLISHING *& Enterprises*, LLC
127 E. Trade Center Terrace
Mustang, Oklahoma 73064 USA